**Learning Services**

**ities**

*a quick guide*

# Gwyneth Hughes & Wendy Smith

**DANIELS PUBLISHING**

# Series Advisers

**Gerald Haigh**  Writer and Consultant in Education

**Pauline Maskell**  Secondary Head of Health Studies

**John Sutton**  General Secretary, Secondary Heads Association

# Advisory Panel

**Ruth Joyce**  Adviser on Drugs and Health Education

**Mike Kirby**  Writer on Education

**Terry Saunders**  Secondary Head of Biology

**Ann Morgan**  Primary Deputy Headteacher

**Elaine Wilson**  Secondary Head of Science

ISBN: 1 85467 303 3

© 1995

While every effort has been made to ensure the accuracy of all statements in this Quick Guide, neither the publisher nor the author can be held responsible for the results of any actions based on such statements. In particular, the Quick Guide is not an authoritative statement of the law, and all quotations from legislation and government guidelines should be checked with the source documents.

Daniels Publishing
38 Cambridge Place
Cambridge CB2 1NS
Tel: 01223 467144  Fax: 01223 467145

# Foreword

I like the idea of Quick Guides. Teachers need reliable information and advice on a very wide range of subjects related to their work and they need it to be accessible and concise. This series attempts to meet those needs by drawing on the knowledge of experienced practitioners and presenting the essential material in a format which facilitates rapid reference and provides valuable action checklists.

I am sure that these guides will be useful to teachers, to governors, to parents and indeed to all who are concerned with the effective management of all aspects of education.

**John Sutton**
General Secretary
Secondary Heads Association

# About the authors

Gwyneth Hughes is a lecturer and researcher at the
University of East London, Stratford, London.

Wendy Smith is a management and consultant trainer
working for Consultancy and Training, Social Services, in
the London Borough of Brent.

# Contents

**Equal Opportunities: a quick guide**

# Introduction

The importance of equal opportunities has increasingly been recognised in education as well as the workplace. It is acknowledged by OFSTED and, although the term 'equal opportunities' is not mentioned, some relevant issues are alluded to in the Parents' Charter. Many schools and colleges now have equal opportunities polices, but in some cases these need to be reviewed. We recognise that much good practice is already occurring in some schools and colleges, and this needs to be extended, reviewed and values. This booklet aims to provide information, teaching strategies, policy statements and review procedures, so that governors, teachers, students and parents can work together to ensure equality exists in practice as well as on paper.

The booklet contains:-

- Background Information
- A checklist of aims and targets for each stage of the planning and implementing an equal opportunities policy.
- A time planner to record progress
- Selected quotations highlighting equality issues and relevant legislation
- Supporting information from the authors' resource pack *Exploring Equal Opportunities*

✓ You may find it useful to tick the boxes when each task is completed.

We would welcome constructive comments on this booklet. Please address them to the publisher.

November 1994

*The term 'equal opportunities' is often used without thinking about what it really means.*

The phrase 'equal opportunities' has become part of our everyday language. It is used in the media, in the workplace and in politics, but often without careful consideration of what the term really means. However, if attention is not paid to the full meaning of equal opportunities, the phrase can become part of an empty rhetoric that pays only lip service to equal opportunities practice.

The rest of this section examines the origins of equal opportunities ideas and the relevant legislation, and considers the concepts of equality and difference.

## The origins of equal opportunities

Equal opportunity as we understand it today has its origins in the feminist and black civil rights movements of the 1950s and 60s. However, equality campaigns have much earlier roots in, for example, the anti-slavery and women's suffrage movements that began in the nineteenth century. The current practice of equal opportunities in the UK follows British equality laws and EC directives, although these are based in part on practice that already existed.

## The legislation

The main relevant pieces of legislation are as follows:

☐ The Sex Discrimination Act 1975

☐ The Race Relations Act 1976

☐ The 1981 Education Act

☐ The **Sex Discrimination Act** makes sex discrimination (against either sex) unlawful in employment, training and education. This means that it is illegal for an educational establishment to discriminate against pupils in its admission process and in its provision of services to pupils. The Act gives individuals the right to direct access to the civil courts and industrial tribunals for legal redress against discrimination. The Equal Opportunities Commission is the body set up to help enforce the legislation and to encourage equal opportunities initiatives.

Exceptions to the Act are allowed where a Genuine Occupational Qualification can be demonstrated, that is where it is necessary to employ a man or a women because of the nature of a particular job. Single sex educational establishments are also allowed under the Act.

*The Sex Discrimination Act is intended to protect both sexes from discrimination.*

**The Race Relations Act aims to protect people from racial discrimination.**

In a similar manner, the **Race Relations Act** makes it unlawful to discriminate against anyone on the grounds of race. It also provides for recourse to the courts. The Act allows persons of a particular racial group access to facilities to meet their particular needs in education, such as English language support. The overseeing body for this Act is the Commission for Racial Equality.

The **1981 Education Act** includes a duty for LEAs to educate children with special educational needs in mainstream schools, where this is reasonably practicable. Staff should be informed about children with special needs. It is the governors' duty to ensure that the school meets an individual's special educational requirements. Parents have the right to appeal against decisions on their child's assessment and on the provision of appropriate education.

## Equality and Difference

Today there is a recognition that equal opportunities practice goes beyond the idea of equal treatment to a positive acknowledgement of difference and diversity. Although an 'equality' approach that treats everyone in the same way attempts to be fair, it does not allow for the fact that individuals do not all start from the same position in society.

*Equal treatment will not achieve equal opportunities when everyone is not equal in the first place.*

Equal treatment does not achieve equal opportunities in a culture where discrimination and stereotyping occur on the grounds of sex, race, class, disability, special educational needs, sexuality, age, culture, religion and financial status. For example, some women are not in a position to take up a job that requires weekend or evening work, because family responsibilities are still not shared equally between the sexes. However, the view that equal treatment is sufficient has been and still is widespread.

A second, more radical, equal opportunities agenda has involved an equal outcomes approach, in which positive or affirmative action is used, for example to increase the number of women or black people in senior positions in an organisation. This approach has given rise to much criticism, especially the accusation that affirmative action leads to the promotion of unsuitable people.

*The recognition and valuing of difference helps to achieve equal opportunities.*

In both these approaches, the recognition of difference and the positive aspects of diversity have been largely missing. A concept of difference does not aim to homogenise groups from a variety of backgrounds and blend them into the mainstream. Rather, with a recognition of difference, a group can retain its own identity but yet be given value and a respected place in society. For example, a minority racial group can maintain its religion and culture without marginalisation or isolation, while playing a full and active part in the community.

Also part of the understanding of difference is the acknowledgement that we are not all the same. Instead of striving to become so, we can enrich our lives by appreciating and learning from the variety of life experiences that surround us. An organisation that is itself able to change and benefit from the diversity of its members, by embracing different cultural perspectives, or by moving beyond traditional gender roles, is the one in which equal opportunities is likely to have a real impact.

Finally, an equal opportunities principle that emphasises diversity should not neglect the equality aspect. It is necessary to move away from hierarchies of difference, such as one in which gender is more important than, say, disability, so that the basis of the equal opportunities concept is equality *and* difference.

# Appreciating the need for equal opportunities strategies

## Aim

To gain an understanding of the need for an equal opportunities strategy

## Targets

Heads, teachers and governors need to:

☐ Develop awareness of equal opportunities legislation.

☐ Initiate discussion on the meaning of equal opportunities at PTA, INSET, staff and governors' meetings.

☐ Identify training needs and support required to proceed with equal opportunities work.

☐ Be aware of individuals and groups in the school who may potentially be experiencing discrimination or stereotyping.

☐ Develop awareness that the issues of equality and difference are relevant to all staff and pupils.

☐ Recognise the importance of equal opportunities, and that time and resources need to be allocated.

'Direct sex discrimination arises where a person treats a woman on the grounds of her sex, less favourably than he (sic) treats, or would treat, a man.'

*(Sex Discrimination Act 1975)*

# Initial Planning and review of existing provision

*Detailed equal opportunities analysis and policy making are best achieved by the formation of a representative working party.*

## Aim

To prepare for the planning process by collecting information already available on equal opportunities practices in the institution and identifying existing good practice.

## Targets

☐ The head teacher and governors should provide resources and appoint a working party to review existing position. The working party should involve parents, governors, teachers, and people from different curricular, administrative and management areas of the school, and there should be a balance of gender, race, culture and age that reflects the composition of the school. The working party should either include student representatives or consult them.

☐ The working party should be issued with a copy of this guide and given a clear brief and instructions on reporting back findings.

☐ The working party should assess the quality of existing equal opportunities policies, if there are any.

☐ The working party should survey existing institutional documentation for equal opportunities statements and relevant statistics (eg staffing, exam entry figures, exam results, option choice groups).

**Equal Opportunities: a quick guide**

☐ The working party should consider comments from LEA Inspectors and OFSTED reports on equal opportunities.

*The working party should involve as many points of view as possible.*

☐ Teachers should provide information for working party on current equal opportunities practice in, for instance, resource selection, classroom practice, subject choices, careers advice, and assessment. Teachers could be asked to identify what is good about existing practice.

☐ Students' views could be canvassed via a special forum, classroom discussions, school council, questionnaire or other appropriate methods.

☐ The governors and PTA should receive a report of the main findings of this review.

# Involving all parents

*'...during the year you will be able to see the work of the school and talk to staff. This will help you find out how your child is being taught and what you can do to help.'*

*(Parents Charter 1994)*

## Aim

To involve parents by communicating relevant information to them and providing a framework for them to participate fully in the school's equal opportunities programme.

## Targets

☐ The PTA and governors should decide in consultation with teachers how to involve parents in the implementation and evaluation of equality and difference practices in all areas of the school.

☐ Ensure that information regarding current equal opportunities initiatives is available to parents, for instance in the school prospectus.

☐ Inform parents of opportunities to see teaching materials and to how these are used in the classroom; set up an open door policy for them to see equal opportunities in practice.

☐ Identify and implement other ways of keeping parents involved and informed, such as open evenings, lesson participation, extra curricular activities, and school management.

☐ Maintain contact with community groups representing parents, especially religious and cultural groups.

# Designing a Framework

## Aim

To discuss and agree a clear framework within which equality and the valuing of difference is integrated into the school.

*A clear framework is essential to the systematic integration of equal opportunities into school life.*

## Targets

The working party should complete the following:

- Discuss what an integrated approach to equality and difference might involve, and agree a working definition that will be acceptable to teachers, parents and pupils.

- Consider the possible links between the school's ethos, that is, its philosophy and aims, and equal opportunities values, so as to build on existing good practice and provide a safer, supportive environment for all, irrespective of sexuality, disability, etc.

'The DfE now requires all LEA and grant-maintained schools to keep ethnic records about their pupils. Further education colleges too, are expected to include ethnic details when they enrol students.'

(Commission for Racial Equality publicity leaflet)

☐ Review the composition and structure of the staff to discover the gender and race balance at different levels and in different areas; review staff recruitment, selection and promotion procedures in the light of these findings. Note that the environment must be supportive to enable lesbians, gay men, and disabled people to identify themselves.

☐ Review the student admission policies and procedures and exclusion figures to ensure that discrimination is not occurring.

☐ Identify desirable values and express these in terms of objectives that the teaching programme would seek to achieve.

☐ Agree the balance to be achieved between didactic methods and a more active student based approach that draws on pupils' own experience.

☐ Present a report to the governors and PTA for discussion and ratification.

# Formulating a Policy

## Aim

To discuss and agree the main elements of an authoritative and thorough policy that will not appear dogmatic or officious.

## Targets

☐ The working party should outline the aims and objectives of the policy, and the rationale for integrating equality and difference procedures into all areas of the school.

☐ The working party, in consultation with relevant others, should agree the principles of curriculum organisation and management and decide who will co-ordinate and evaluate the integration of equality and difference practices. Although this should be everyone's responsibility, it is valuable to have one or two designated co-ordinators.

*Consultation with governors, teachers, parents and students will encourage people to feel the policy belongs to them, and thus promote its successful implementation.*

**The policy needs to be reviewed and updated regularly.**

☐ The working party, in consultation with relevant others, should agree the principles of staff and student selection, and establish what statistical information will be required.

☐ The teaching staff should produce an outline of the curriculum content and make recommendations about teaching methods and any statistical information needed, for instance, on assessment levels or exam results.

☐ Agree procedures to be used in the event of complaints of discrimination.

☐ Identify opportunities for co-operation between teachers and parents in supporting the diverse educational needs of pupils.

☐ Agree a mechanism for allowing governors, teachers and parents to review teaching materials and methods, anti-discriminatory action and staff and student selection procedures.

# Writing a Policy Document

## Aim

To prepare a policy document that is freely available for students, parents, teachers and others to consult.

## Targets

- The working party should produce a draft policy, including details of implementing and evaluating the following:
  - the rationale for ensuring equal opportunity and valuing difference in the school.
  - the aims and objectives of integrating equality and difference.
  - the equality framework.
  - the principles of curriculum organisation and management.
  - teaching methods and classroom management.
  - the outline of curriculum content.
  - the procedure to be employed in the event of a complaint of discrimination by pupils, parents or staff; a pro-forma reporting sheet could be used (see Appendix).
  - recruitment and promotion of staff in accordance with the policy.
  - recruitment of students and provision of courses for all abilities and capabilities in the sixth form.
  - procedures to monitor relevant statistics, and action to be taken if any group is found to be under- or over-represented among students or staff, relative to the community at large, or problems arise concerning equality and difference.

*A policy document needs to be clear and comprehensive and contain strategies for ensuring that the policy is put into practice.*

*Everyone needs to be able to read the document.*

☐ Arrange wider consultation with all parents, teachers, students and governors.

☐ Review the draft policy in the light of feedback from parents, teachers, students and governors.

☐ Produce a policy document with consideration for readers' needs; it should be in language appropriate for students, available in Braille or large print as necessary, and translated into local community languages.

☐ Ensure accessible distribution of the policy document in staff bases, form rooms and year rooms, and to all staff, parents and governors.

# Involving students in equal opportunities

## Aim

To ensure that all students understand the concept of equal opportunities and feel fully involved.

## Targets

- Ensure that students understand the concept of equal opportunities, through group work or class discussion.

- Ensure that students understand the concept of difference and can give examples that demonstrate the inadequacy of the 'equality only' approach (see Background Information, page 00).

- Encourage students to appreciate that equal opportunities are also their responsibility.

- Discuss and obtain feedback on policy documents, if this is appropriate for their age group.

- Initiate project work, debates, open discussions and display work on the theme of equal opportunities.

- Empower students to deal with any discrimination they encounter themselves; encourage them to talk to parents or teachers and use appropriate formal complaint procedures where necessary.

*Open and frank discussion with students is vital, because silence is collusion with discrimination.*

*'Your child has the right to broad and balanced studies which promote spiritual, moral, cultural, mental and physical development, and prepare him or her for adult life.'*

*(Parents' Charter 1994)*

## Aim

To ensure all teachers include equal opportunities in curriculum content.

NB It might be thought that some of the targets below require extra work. However, much good practice can be achieved by integrating equal opportunities practice into daily work. We recommend requesting INSET and release from other duties where this is needed.

## Targets

- Teachers check all resources used for discriminatory material, such as sexist, racist, prejudiced, classist or ableist language and stereotypes, or negative images or non-representation of groups that face discrimination. (See Supporting Material and Glossary, pages 00–00)
- If discriminatory material is found, either replace it or else use the material as a chance to raise issues of equality and difference with the class.
- Write or purchase new resource material that shows differences in a positive light and challenges discrimination.
- Ensure the curriculum reflects cultural and religious diversity, both within the school and in society at large, and emphasises this wherever possible within the National Curriculum.
- Encourage students to include their own cultural perspective in their work.
- Encourage students to recognise the benefits of including different cultural perspectives in their work, to give a richer and more complete view, eg the contribution of women and black people to science and literature.

# Equal opportunities and teaching methods

## Aim

To ensure that classroom practice reflects an equal opportunities approach.

*Equal opportunities must exist in practice as well as on paper to be effective.*

## Targets

- [ ] Consider individual pupils' educational needs, not just those with recognised special educational needs, but also needs arising from their race, gender etc. It is important not to make negative assumptions, for instance that only girls lack confidence in science or maths or that students with physical disabilities have learning difficulties.
- [ ] Check your assessment results for bias in methods or materials against any group of students. Investigate the causes and try to remedy them, for instance under-achievement by boys.
- [ ] Consider your classroom practice: do all students get a fair share of attention, time and resources? If not, take steps to redress this.
- [ ] Experiment with different teaching methods to find out which are more favourably received.
- [ ] Check that neither you nor the students use discriminatory language, such the use of 'Mankind' to mean the whole human race, the word 'black' in a negative context, or phrases that assume everyone is able bodied, such as 'stand on your own two feet'. Rather than just correcting inappropriate language, use it as an opportunity to discuss the issues. (see Supporting Information, page 00)
- [ ] Deal with conflict arising out of differences between groups of pupils, and ensure discriminatory behaviour does not pass unchallenged. Encourage student initiatives to eliminate group conflict and oppose discrimination.

# Dealing with resistance and opposition to equal opportunities initiatives

'Where a child who has special educational needs is being educated in an ordinary school maintained by a local authority it shall be the duty of those concerned with making special educational provision to secure...that the child engages in the activities of the school together with children who not have special educational needs.'

(1981 Education Act)

## Aim

To use possible conflict constructively.

## Targets

☐ Ensure you have a clear understanding of equality and difference issues and a knowledge of the institution's policy.

☐ Use resistance and conflict (such as racist or sexist insults or the bullying of students with special educational needs) as an opportunity to address and discuss equal opportunities.

☐ Explain the institution's policy clearly and calmly to anyone whose behaviour suggests they do not understand it.

☐ Request INSET to practice or role play dealing with conflict, for example that arising from differences associated with religious beliefs, gender issues and sexuality.

☐ Request INSET, PTA meetings, or governors' training to raise awareness of specific equality and difference issues.

☐ Modify policy and practice to take account of constructive criticisms arising out of any conflict and consequent discussion.

**Equal Opportunities: a quick guide**

# Implementing procedures for monitoring and evaluation

## Aim

To ensure that the agreed equal opportunities integration is happening effectively.

## Targets

- [ ] The working party (or appointed individuals) should monitor the effectiveness of the planning and organisational procedures that have been established.

- [ ] Teachers should devise and implement procedures for evaluating how well equality integration has taken place, and to recommend changes if necessary.

- [ ] Mechanisms should be identified for encouraging and responding to feedback from parents, for instance from discussions at parents' groups or PTA meetings.

- [ ] Procedures should be established for encouraging and responding to feedback from students, eg from group discussions, questionnaires or evaluation forms.

- [ ] Arrangements should be made for an annual progress report to the governing body and PTA.

*Governors, parents, students and teachers all need to be involved in monitoring equality and understanding differences, to ensure that equal opportunities works in practice.*

# Supporting information 1: Stereotyping

*Our expectations are conditioned by stereotypes much more than we realise.*

The following pages are based on the authors' teaching resource pack *Exploring Equal Opportunities*, which contains many ideas for activities, discussion and projects that can be used in equal opportunities work in class.

☐ Stereotyping occurs when certain groups of people, such as disabled, black, males, females or older people, are assumed to have particular characteristics. These assumptions are based on prejudice rather than fact.

Consider the following riddle:

☐ A father and his son were involved in a road accident. The father was killed and his son badly injured. The son was rushed to hospital and was immediately admitted to the operating theatre. The surgeon looked shocked and exclaimed 'That's my son on the operating table!'

How is this possible?

☐ This riddle usually puzzles people for a while because we expect the surgeon to be male, and therefore to be the boy's father, who we know is dead. Of course, the answer is that the surgeon is the boy's mother. We don't expect the surgeon to be a woman because women are stereotyped as being caring and supportive, as a nurse might be, but not capable of a high-powered, pressurised job such as a surgeon's.

Stereotyping does not only affect the jobs we chooses, but also influences all aspects of our lives. From an early age, conditioning encourages us to behave in a way society considers appropriate, whether as black, white, female, male, disabled, or whatever. However, people do resist being stereotyped. Organisations such as the Commission for Racial Equality carry out research to counter stereotypes of black people, and some individuals make concerted efforts not to be stereotyped themselves. (This, of course, creates another type of pressure.)

*Even 'positive' stereotypes are restricting.*

### Why is stereotyping a problem?

Stereotyping is damaging because it restricts people's life choices. For instance, women may not feel it is appropriate to aim at a career as a surgeon. It is important to realise that even a statement which appears very positive, like 'Asian pupils are quiet and hard-working at school', is as much a stereotype as a negative statement like 'older people are forgetful'. Positive stereotypes cause problems because people are under pressure to live up to the stereotype, for instance to perform well at school.

**The language we use influences the way we think about people.**

☐ Discriminatory language perpetuates stereotypes about groups of people. For example, men have been stereotyped as strong and powerful, and as breadwinners, while women have been stereotyped as weak or attractive, and as wives or home-makers. Discrimination also includes biased or negative representations of groups of people, such as black people being portrayed as criminals, or disabled people as not being intelligent.

☐ Language may be discriminatory if it implies that the white, able-bodied male is the norm. Words like 'he', or 'mankind', being used to include both sexes are examples of this, or the use of words like 'vision' that assume everyone can see.

☐ Any language that presents the viewpoint of more powerful groups in society and does not include the experiences of less powerful groups is also discriminatory.

☐ Non-discriminatory language does not contain the obvious discrimination described above. This is avoided by using, for instance, gender-neutral words such as 'people', 'student' or 'chairperson'. However, non-discriminatory language does not challenge the inequalities that exist in our society.

**Equal Opportunities: a quick guide**

Anti-discriminatory language does challenge discrimination. This can be done by using positive images of people who have historically been discriminated against.

*Alternatives can easily be found for negative words containing 'black', for instance.*

Anti-discriminatory language specifically uses 'she' instead of, or as well as 'he', or ensures that the word 'black' is not used in a negative way, as in the phrase 'Black Monday'. It will include the experiences of less powerful groups and acknowledge and respect the valuable contributions that all people make to society.

## Why discrimination in language matters.

Many words containing 'black' have a negative association, while words containing 'white' are positive or neutral. This could be disputed over the word 'whitewash', which is sometimes quoted as an example of negative association. However, using 'whitewash' to mean a cover-up implies that white is positive and gives a clean appearance to something negative or unpleasant like a scandal.

The presentation of black as negative can undermine the identity and self-esteem of black people, as well as perpetuating the racist view that white is superior to black. Alternative phrases can easily be found, such as 'extortion' instead of 'blackmail', or 'illegal trade' instead of 'black market'.

# Time Planner

| Stage | Completed by | tick box |
|---|---|---|
| Agree a plan for developing/amending equal opportunities policy | | ☐ |
| Set up a working party with responsibility for writing the policy – allow time for the work to be done. | | ☐ |
| Review existing provision | | ☐ |
| Establish wider parental involvement | | ☐ |
| Identify a framework | | ☐ |
| Produce draft policy | | ☐ |
| Involve students | | ☐ |
| Consultation and feedback | | ☐ |
| Revise draft policy | | ☐ |
| Distribute policy | | ☐ |
| Integrate issues of equality and difference into all aspects of the school/college | | ☐ |

# Glossary

| | |
|---|---|
| **Ableism** | Prejudice against a group of people because of what they cannot do with their bodies or minds. It is the result of too little awareness of the experience of those with disabilities. |
| **Able-bodied** | People who are not disabled. |
| **Ageism** | Prejudice against people because of their age. The belief that they are unable to take care of themselves, or lack the necessary experience, or are too old to learn new skills. |
| **Ambulism** | The assumption that everyone can walk without difficulty. |
| **Black** | Defined by black people themselves not only by skin colour but also by specific experiences of discrimination. 'Black' as a political term encompasses people from different racial groups who suffer from racism. |
| **Classism** | Prejudice against a social class, in which the values of one class are imposed on another. For instance, working-class people are seen by middle-class and upper-class people as ignorant, stupid, coarse and ineffectual. |
| **Closeted** | Applied to lesbians and gay men, it means that they keep their sexuality hidden for fear of persecution. |
| **Come** out | To declare one's sexuality. Lesbians and gay men who have kept their sexuality secret for fear of prejudice may make a decision to come out so that they can live a whole life, not a double one, but such a decision requires great courage. |
| **Discrimination** | Selection, different treatment, especially on grounds of sex, race, religion, sexuality or disability. Discrimination can in theory be favourable or unfavourable, but the word is usually used in a negative sense. See 'Positive discrimination'. |

| | |
|---|---|
| **Feminist** | Someone who, in a male-dominated society, works towards the equality of women with men. 'I myself have never been able to find out precisely what feminism is: I only know that people call me a feminist when I express sentiments which differentiate me from a doormat' – Rebecca West (1913). |
| **Gay** | In the 1960s, the term 'gay' was taken up as an alternative to 'homosexual' by the Gay Liberation Movement to affirm 'a truly joyous alternative lifestyle'. It is used predominantly of homosexual men, as in 'Lesbian and Gay Pride Festival'. |
| **Heterosexism** | The assumption that only heterosexuality is normal or natural, and that anyone homosexual is sick, perverted, or in need of help. |
| **Heterosexual** | Someone who is attracted physically and emotionally to the opposite sex. |
| **Homophobia** | A fear of homosexuality. Also a prejudice against homosexual people. 'Homo-' in 'homosexuality' means 'same', but because it also means 'man', 'homophobia' is usually interpreted as meaning prejudice against gay men. |
| **Homosexual** | Someone who is physically and emotionally attracted to their own sex. Like 'homophobia', it is more often applied to gay men than to lesbians, for the same reason. |
| **Lesbian** | A woman who is physically and emotionally attracted to other women. |
| **Multicultural** | This should mean containing or belonging to many cultures, but it is often used to mean 'not of the dominant culture'. It is also used to replace such terms as 'anti-racist', but this is not correct either. |
| **Oppression** | The practice of treating people cruelly or unjustly, overwhelming or distressing them. |

| | |
|---|---|
| **Positive discrimination** | The attempt to counter negative discrimination by favouring women, ethnic minorities or other oppressed groups in, for instance, appointment or promotion policies. |
| **Prejudice** | A judgement formed beforehand without proper knowledge, usually unfavourable. When prejudiced people have power, the result is discrimination, for instance by men against women. |
| **Racism** | Discrimination, prejudice or oppression based on race or ethnic identity. |
| **Sexism** | Discrimination, prejudice or oppression based on gender. Since power has traditionally rested with men, sexism is usually directed at women. |
| **Stereotyping** | The assumption that a person will have certain characteristics because they belong to a certain group. It is usually based on ignorance or fear. |
| **Anti- and Non-** | These prefixes are applied to many of the above terms. 'Anti-' is an active term, implying that discrimination is being challenged, whereas 'non-' usually has a passive sense, that discrimination is merely avoided. For instance, a non-racist person would not display racist behaviour, but might not go out of their way to challenge racism, whereas an anti-racist person would use every opportunity to challenge it. |

# Racist incident reporting sheet*

No racist incident can be ignored. All racist incidents must be formally reported.

The minimum response consistent with action associated with other serious disciplinary matters is indicated by the empty boxes. The boxes should be initialled and ticked when that action is completed.

Extra information may be added on the reverse of the sheet, eg, if staff do not follow the course of responses above, to indicate why.

The purpose of the sheet is to provide a formal record of the incident and of the teachers's actions. It does not replace the normal communications channels amongst teachers involved in dealing with any disciplinary matter. The sheet should be returned to the teacher with designated responsibility for multicultural/anti-racist matters when the incident is closed. The incident sheet will be available for inspection by the governors and any authorised person or group.

*used by permission of Hinchingbrooke School, Huntingdon

**Equal Opportunities: a quick guide**

# Racist incident reporting sheet

Date .........................

Teacher ....................

Pupil .........................

Form .........................

| Category | Discussion with pupil | Form tutor informed | Referral to HOD or HOH | Formal discussion: pupil, staff | Letter to parents/guardians | Interview with parents/guardians | Pupil to be excluded/sent home | Request to governors for suspension |
|---|---|---|---|---|---|---|---|---|
| **1 Verbal abuse** | | | | | | | | |
| Incidental, no offence intended | | ▓ | ▓ | ▓ | ▓ | ▓ | ▓ | ▓ |
| Persistent, intended to be offensive | | | | | | ▓ | ▓ | ▓ |
| Inciting others | | | | | | | ▓ | ▓ |
| Vicious/threatening | | | | | | | | |
| **2 Refusal to co-operate** | | | | | | | | |
| Sit next to/talk to/work with/help | | | | ▓ | ▓ | ▓ | ▓ | ▓ |
| Persistent | | | | | | | ▓ | ▓ |
| **3 Violence** | | | | | | | | |
| Jostling | | ▓ | ▓ | ▓ | ▓ | ▓ | | |
| Intimidation | | | | | | ▓ | ▓ | |
| Vicious fighting | | | | | | | | ▓ |
| Use of weapons | | | | | | | | |
| **4 Abuse of personal property** | | | | | | ▓ | ▓ | |
| **5 Graffiti** | | | | ▓ | ▓ | ▓ | ▓ | |
| **6 Racist propaganda** | | | | | | ▓ | ▓ | ▓ |

Equal Opportunities Commission
Overseas House
Quay Street
Manchester M3 3HN
telephone 0161 833-9244

Commission for Racial Equality
Elliot House
10-12 Allington Street
London SW1E 5EH
telephone 0171 828-7022

Spinal Injuries Association
New Point House
76, St James Lane
Muswell Hill
London N10 3DF
counselling line 0181 883-4296

Department for Education
Sanctuary Buildings
Great Smith Street
London SW1P 3BT
telephone 0171 925-5555

Further Education Unit
Citadel Place
Tinworth Street
London SE11 5EH
telephone 0171 962-1280

Blackliners
Unit 46, Eurolink Business Centre
49 Effra Road
London SW2 1BH
telephone 0171 738-5274

ChildLine
Royal Mail Building
50 Studd Street
London N1 0QW
(Office) 0171 239-1000
(Helpline) 0800 1111

National Association for Pastoral Care In Education
Institute of Education
University of Warwick
Coventry CV4 7AL
01203 523810

National Association of Young People's Counselling and
Advisory Services
send sae for local details to:
NAYPCAS
Magazine Business Centre
11 Newarke Street
Leicester LE1 5SF
telephone 01533 559711

Royal Association in Aid of Deaf People (RAD)
27 Old Oak Road
Acton
London W3 7HN
telephone 0181 743-6187

Your local authority has an Equal Opportunities Officer,
and your LEA may have an adviser or advisory teacher
for equal opportunities. Contact the authority's main
switchboard to get in touch with them.

# Resources

The Further Education Unit (FEU) produces several documents on gender, race and disability.

G Anonouris and J Wilson, *Equal Opportunities in Schools*, Cassell 1989.

Madeleine Arnot, ed., *Race and Gender: equal opportunities policies in education*, The Open University Press 1985.

Susan Askew and Carol Ross, *Boys Don't Cry: boys and sexism in education*, Open University Press 1988.

Godfrey L Brandt, *The Realization of Anti-Racist Teaching*, Falmer 1986.

Helen Burchell and Val Millman, *Changing Perspectives on Gender*, Open University Press 1988.

Hilary Claire *et al.*, eds, *Equality Matters: case studies from the primary school*, Multilingual Matters 1993.

Commission for Racial Equality, *Ethnic Monitoring in Education*, 1992.

Debbie Epstein, ed., *Challenging Lesbian and Gay Inequalities in Education*, Open University Press 1994.

Equal Opportunities Commission, *Do You Provide Equal Educational Opportunities? a guide to good practice*, 1983.

John Evans and Brian Davies, eds, *Equality, Education and Physical Education*, Falmer 1993.

Carrie M H Herbert, *Countering Sexual Harassment,* Daniels Publishing 1993.

Carrie M H Herbert, *Sexual Harassment in Schools,* David Fulton 1992.

Gwyneth Hughes and Wendy Smith, *Exploring Equal Opportunities,* Daniels Publishing 1993.

Carol Jones and Pat Mahoney, *Learning our Lines: sexuality and social control in education,* Women's Press 1989.

Anna S King and Michael J Reiss, *The Multicultural Dimension of the National Curriculum,* Falmer 1993.

Michael Kirby, *Rights and Responsibilities,* Daniels Publishing 1993.

Gillian Klein, *Education Towards Race Equality,* Cassell 1993.

Catherine Marshall, ed., *The New Politics of Race and Gender,* Falmer 1994.

Jean Rudduck, *Developing a Gender Policy in Secondary Schools,* Open University Press 1993.

J Swann, *Girls, Boys and Language,* Blackwell 1992.

Sue Dyson and Tricia Szirom, *Greater Expectations: a sourcebook for working with girls and young women,* British edition edited by Hazel Slavin, LDA 1986.

Judith Whyte *et al., Girl-friendly Schooling,* Routledge 1990.

**Equal Opportunities: a quick guide**

## Exploring Equal Opportunities
Gwyneth Hughes and Wendy Smith
ISBN 1 85467 204 5

## Countering Sexual Harassment
Carrie M H Herbert
ISBN 1 85467 213 4

## Developing Assertiveness Skills  second edition
Chrissie Hawkes-Whitehead
ISBN 1 85467 212 6

## Get That Job!
Patricia McBride
ISBN 1 85467 167 7

## How to Interview
Patricia McBride
ISBN 1 85467 166 9

## Raising Self–Esteem: 50 activities
Murray White
ISBN 1 85467 231 2

## Self–Esteem, Its Meaning and Value in Schools, A and B
Murray White
ISBN 1 85467 141 3 and 1 85467 142 1

## Rights and Responsibilities
Michael Kirby
ISBN 1 85467 187 1

## Streetwise: Education for Citizenship
Michael Kirby
ISBN 1 85467 160 X

**Daniels Publishing resource packs are:**

✓ **Fully photocopiable**

✓ **Ready for use**

✓ **Flexible**

✓ **Clearly designed**

✓ **Tried and tested**

✓ **Cost-effective**

# The Quick Guide series from Daniels Publishing

Quick Guides are up to date, stimulating and readable A5 booklets, packed with essential information and key facts on important issues in education

## Class and school management

**Bullying: A Quick Guide**
Dr Carrie Herbert
ISBN 1 85467 301 7

**School Inspections:**
**A Quick Guide**
Malcolm Massey
ISBN 1 85467 308 4

**Grief, Loss and Bereavement:**
**A Quick Guide**
Penny Casdagli & Francis Gobey
ISBN 1 85467 307 6

**Safety on Educational Visits:**
**A Quick Guide**
Michael Evans
ISBN 1 85467 306 8

**Equal Opportunities:**
**A Quick Guide**
Gwyneth Hughes & Wendy Smith
ISBN 1 85467 303 3

**Working in Groups:**
**A Quick Guide**
Pauline Maskell
ISBN 1 85467 304 1

## Career enhancement

**Assertiveness: A Quick Guide**
Chrissie Hawkes-Whitehead
ISBN 1 85467 305 X

**Counselling: A Quick Guide**
Chrissie Hawkes-Whitehead
and Cherry Eales
ISBN 1 85467 302 5

## Health education

**Drugs Education for children**
**aged 4–11: A Quick Guide**
Janice Slough
ISBN 1 85467 310 6

**Drugs Education for children**
**aged 11–18: A Quick Guide**
Janice Slough
ISBN 1 85467 311 4

**Alcohol: A Quick Guide**
Dr Gerald Beales
ISBN 1 85467 300 9

**Smoking Issues: A Quick Guide**
Paul Hooper
ISBN 1 85467 309 2

**Sex Education:**
**A Quick Guide for Teachers**
Dr Michael Kirby
ISBN 1 85467 228 2

**Sex Education for children**
**aged 4–11: A Quick Guide**
**for parents and carers**
Janice Slough
ISBN 1 85467 312 2

**Sex Education for children**
**aged 11–18: A Quick Guide**
**for parents and carers**
Janice Slough
ISBN 1 85467 313 0

For further details of any of our publications mentioned in this Quick Guide, please fill in and post this form (or a photocopy) to:

Daniels Publishing
38 Cambridge Place          Tel: 01223 467144
Cambridge CB2 1NS           Fax: 01223 467145

**Name** ................................................................................................

**Job Title** ..........................................................................................

**Organisation** ...................................................................................

**Address** ...........................................................................................

....................................................................................................

**Postcode** ........................................................................................

**Tel No.** ............................................................................................

**Fax No.** ...........................................................................................

☐ **Please send me details of the following publications:**

☐ **Please keep me informed of forthcoming Quick Guides and other Health Education Resources from Daniels Publishing**

**Have you ordered from us before?** ☐ **No** ☐ **Yes: account no** ...............

# Notes

**Equal Opportunities: a quick guide**

# Notes

# Notes

**Equal Opportunities: a quick guide**